Sports Records

Hockey Records

by Anthony K. Hewson

FOCUS READERS®

BEACON

www.focusreaders.com

Focus Readers is distributed by North Star Editions:
sales@northstareditions.com | 888-417-0195

Produced for Focus Readers by Red Line Editorial.

Photographs ©: Wa Funches/AP Images, cover, 1; Eric Draper/AP Images, 4, 7; Mark Humphrey/AP Images, 8, 29; AP Images, 11, 14, 26–27; Paul Chiasson/AP Images, 13; The Canadian Press/AP Images, 17; Kennedy/AP Images, 19; Duncan Williams/Cal Sport Media/AP Images, 20; Louis Lopez/Cal Sport Media/AP Images, 22; Alvan Quinn/AP Images, 25

Library of Congress Cataloging-in-Publication Data
Names: Hewson, Anthony K., author.
Title: Hockey records / by Anthony K. Hewson.
Description: Lake Elmo : Focus Readers, [2021] | Series: Sports records | Includes index. | Audience: Grades 4-6
Identifiers: LCCN 2020003998 (print) | LCCN 2020003999 (ebook) | ISBN 9781644933626 (Hardcover) | ISBN 9781644934388 (Paperback) | ISBN 9781644935149 (eBook) | ISBN 9781644935903 (PDF)
Subjects: LCSH: Hockey--Records--Juvenile literature. | Sports records--Juvenile literature.
Classification: LCC GV847.5 .H49 2021 (print) | LCC GV847.5 (ebook) | DDC 796.962--dc23
LC record available at https://lccn.loc.gov/2020003998
LC ebook record available at https://lccn.loc.gov/2020003999

Printed in the United States of America
Mankato, MN
082020

About the Author

Anthony K. Hewson is a freelance writer, originally from San Diego, now living in the Bay Area with his wife and their two dogs.

Table of Contents

99
EASTON
supra
CCM

Chapter 1

A New Goal King

Wayne Gretzky grew up in the 1960s. He was a big fan of Gordie Howe. Many people said Howe was the greatest hockey player ever.

In 1994, there was a challenger for the title of greatest player ever.

Wayne Gretzky warms up before a 1994 game against the Vancouver Canucks.

It was Gretzky. He was chasing Howe's biggest record. Howe had scored 801 goals in his National Hockey League (NHL) **career**. And Gretzky had tied the record. He needed one more goal to break it.

Gretzky received a pass. Then he fired the puck at the net. It was goal 802. Gretzky was the new

Gretzky played against Howe in 1979. Howe was 50 years old. Gretzky was 18.

Wayne Gretzky scores the 802nd goal of his career.

goal king. By the end of his career, Gretzky had broken several more of Howe's records.

99
HESPE
HESPELER

Chapter 2

The Great One

Most hockey fans agree that Wayne Gretzky was the greatest player ever. He played 20 seasons in the NHL. During that time, he set or tied more than 60 records.

Wayne Gretzky played on four different NHL teams during his career.

Gretzky became known as "The Great One."

Gretzky was not the biggest player on the ice. But he was a talented skater. He always seemed to know where the puck was going.

During the 1981–82 season, Gretzky scored 92 goals. He broke the old record of 76. Gretzky ended his NHL career with 894 goals. That's another record.

Gretzky was also a great passer. He racked up 1,963 **assists**. In

Gretzky helped the Edmonton Oilers win four Stanley Cups.

total, he had 2,857 career **points**. No other player has more than 2,000 points.

Gretzky set his favorite record during the 1981–82 season.

On December 30, 1981, he scored his 50th goal of the season. It happened during the season's 39th game. Gretzky became the fastest player to score 50 goals in a season. Before Gretzky, only two players had scored 50 goals in 50 games. But Gretzky beat their mark by 11 games.

The longest Gretzky ever went without a point was four games.

Gretzky joined the Hockey Hall of Fame in 2000.

Gretzky played his last game in 1999. He received a huge honor. The NHL **retired** his No. 99 jersey. Nobody will ever wear that number on the ice again.

NORTHLAND

Chapter 3

Tremendous Teams

One of the NHL's top teams has been around since the beginning. The Montreal Canadiens were founded in 1909. That was eight years before the NHL even existed.

Jean Beliveau (left) played with the Canadiens his entire career. He helped the team win 10 Stanley Cups.

The Canadiens are the oldest pro hockey team in the world.

The Canadiens have also won the most Stanley Cups. The team's greatest era was 1956 to 1960. Montreal won five Stanley Cups in a row. No other team has done that since.

Henri Richard won the Stanley Cup 11 times with the Canadiens. That is the most of any player.

Each year, the Stanley Cup is engraved with the winning team's name and the players' names.

From 1976 to 1979, the Canadiens won another four. The 1976–77 team may have been the best ever. Nine Hall of Famers played for Montreal that season.

They scored the most goals of any team. They also gave up the fewest goals of any team. That season, the Canadiens lost only eight games.

Fierce Flyers

The 1979–80 Philadelphia Flyers were tough. And no other NHL team has ever had an undefeated streak

The 1974–75 Washington Capitals won just eight games. That set a record for fewest wins.

Bobby Clarke (16) was a big scorer for the Flyers during their undefeated streak.

like theirs. On October 13, 1979, the Flyers lost a game. They didn't lose their next 35 games. That 35-game undefeated streak set an all-time record.

SHER-WOOD
30
SHER-WOOD
T100
SHER-WOOD
CANADA

Chapter 4

Colossal Careers

From 1993 to 2014, there was one thing the New Jersey Devils didn't have to worry about. They knew who was going to be in goal. Martin Brodeur was one of the greatest goalies ever.

Martin Brodeur had 125 shutouts during his career. That is an NHL record.

Martin Brodeur played with the New Jersey Devils for 21 seasons.

Brodeur won a record 691 games in his career. He is the only goalie to win 600 or more. Brodeur was more than a great goalie. He was also reliable. For 10 seasons in a row, Brodeur played in 70 or more games. That record should be safe for a while. In the 2018–19 season, not a single goalie played 70 games.

Penalty King

David Williams was known as "Tiger." Williams could score goals. But he was more famous for his fists. Williams was an **enforcer**. His physical play earned him 3,971 **penalty minutes** in his career.

As of 2020, no **active** player even had half as many.

Mr. Hockey

Gordie Howe began his NHL career in 1946. And he didn't stop playing until 1980. In fact, Howe is the oldest person to ever play in an NHL game. Howe was 52 years

Gordie Howe returned to pro hockey in 1997. He was 69 years old. He played one game for the minor-league Detroit Vipers.

Gordie Howe steals the puck from a New York Rangers player during a 1963 game.

old when he retired. He played for 32 seasons. In total, Howe played 1,767 NHL games. He set the record for most games played.

Mr. Goalie

NHL goalies don't play every game anymore. Even the best ones get days off to rest. That was not the case when Glenn Hall played. Hall is known as Mr. Goalie.

Hall played his first NHL game in 1952. He became the **starter** for the Detroit Red Wings in 1955. He played every game for two seasons. Then he was traded to the Chicago Black Hawks. But Hall kept his streak going. He didn't take a night off until 1962. That was a record streak of 502 games.

Hall made 24,611 saves in 16 NHL seasons.

FOCUS ON
Hockey Records

Write your answers on a separate piece of paper.

1. Write a paragraph summarizing Wayne Gretzky's career.

2. Which NHL record do you think will be the hardest to break? Why?

3. Which team has won the most Stanley Cups?

- **A.** New Jersey Devils
- **B.** Montreal Canadiens
- **C.** Philadelphia Flyers

4. Why is Howe's record for oldest NHL player unlikely to be broken?

- **A.** No player has ever been as good as Howe.
- **B.** Most players' bodies wear out by their 40s.
- **C.** Hockey is more violent than it used to be.

5. What does **challenger** mean in this book?

*In 1994, there was a **challenger** for the title of greatest player ever. It was Gretzky. He was chasing Howe's biggest record.*

- **A.** a person who is not good at what he does
- **B.** a person who holds an important record
- **C.** a person who tries to beat someone else

6. What does **era** mean in this book?

*The team's greatest **era** was 1956 to 1960. Montreal won five Stanley Cups in a row.*

- **A.** a period of time
- **B.** an important win
- **C.** a famous team

Answer key on page 32.

Glossary

active
Still playing in a league.

assists
Passes that lead directly to a teammate scoring a goal.

career
The total amount of time that an athlete plays his or her sport.

enforcer
A hockey player who defends his teammates by fighting members of the other team.

penalty minutes
Time a player must spend off the ice after breaking a rule.

points
The number of goals a player scores plus the number of assists the player has.

retired
Decided that a jersey number may no longer be worn by another player.

starter
A player who participates in a game from its beginning.

To Learn More

BOOKS

Fishman, Jon M. *Hockey's G.O.A.T.: Wayne Gretzky, Sidney Crosby, and More.* Minneapolis: Lerner Publications, 2020.

Frederick, Shane. *Hockey's Record Breakers.* North Mankato, MN: Capstone Press, 2017.

Morey, Allan. *Hockey Records.* Minneapolis: Bellwether Media, 2018.

NOTE TO EDUCATORS

Visit **www.focusreaders.com** to find lesson plans, activities, links, and other resources related to this title.

Index

Answer Key: 1. Answers will vary; **2.** Answers will vary; **3.** B; **4.** B; **5.** C; **6.** A